THE BEST
CAT MEMES
EVER

D0888147

THE BEST CAT MEMES EVER

An Hachette UK Company
www.hachette.co.uk

Summersdale Publishers Ltd
Part of Octopus Publishing Group Limited
Carmelite House
50 Victoria Embankment
LONDON
EC4Y 0DZ
UK

www.summersdale.com

Printed and bound in China

ISBN: 978-1-78685-784-2

Substantial discounts on bulk quantities of Summersdale books are available to corporations, professional associations and other organizations. For details contact general enquiries: telephone: +44 (0) 1243 771107 or email: enquiries@summersdale.com.

THE BEST
CAT MEMES
EVER

When you
remember that
awkward thing
you did eight
years ago

summersdale

WHEN YOU FAKE HAVING PLANS SO YOU CAN STAY IN AND CHILL

THEM: JUST BE NORMAL
ME:

WHEN THE PHOTOGRAPHER SAYS "JUST SMILE NATURALLY" AND YOU FORGET WHAT NATURAL IS

TRIPLE-CHECKING YOUR SOCIAL MEDIA PROFILES TO SEE HOW THEY LOOK TO YOUR CRUSH

SETTING YOUR ALARM AND CALCULATING HOW MANY HOURS, MINUTES AND SECONDS OF SLEEP YOU'RE GOING TO GET TONIGHT

WHEN YOU GET CAUGHT
PRACTISING DANCE
MOVES IN PRIVATE

WHEN SOMEONE'S HAVING A PRIVATE
CONVERSATION AND YOU KNOW
YOU SHOULDN'T EAVESDROP

WAITER: ENJOY
YOUR MEAL
ME: YOU TOO

REGARDS

WHEN YOU SEE THE PERFECT MEME AND
HAVE TO TAG A FRIEND IMMEDIATELY

WHEN YOU DON'T HEAR WHAT SOMEONE SAID AND YOU JUST TRY TO LAUGH IT OFF

WHEN YOU'RE HOME ALONE AND YOU
CAN DO WHATEVER YOU WANT

TRAVELLING IN THE PASSENGER SEAT AND PRETENDING TO BE IN A MOODY MUSIC VIDEO

WHEN YOU SHOW YOUR FRIEND A VIDEO AND HAVE TO CHECK THEY'RE FINDING IT FUNNY

THE FEELING WHEN YOUR CRUSH LIKES YOUR POST

MY FACE WHEN I FORGET WHETHER I LEFT THE STRAIGHTENERS ON

WHEN YOU GOOGLE YOUR SYMPTOMS AND DISCOVER THAT YOU HAVE SIX INCURABLE DISEASES AND A WEEK TO LIVE

ME: *SENDS PICTURE TO CRUSH*

ME: OOPS HAHA WRONG PERSON

GOING TO WORK ON
MONDAY MORNING

BAE: YOU LOOK GREAT TODAY

ME:

ME: NEW YEAR, NEW ME
ME 5 SECONDS LATER:

WHEN YOU'VE GOT SOME SERIOUS GOSS TO UNLEASH ON THE REST OF THE GROUP

THEM: CAN I HAVE A
VOLUNTEER PLEASE?
ME:

ME MAKING PLANS
TO GO OUT

PRETENDING TO BE SURPRISED WHEN SOMEONE TELLS YOU A SECRET, EVEN THOUGH YOU ALREADY WORKED IT OUT WEEKS AGO

WHEN YOU'RE WALKING IN TIME TO YOUR MUSIC

WHEN SOMEONE REPEATS THE SAME THING YOU SAID 20 MINUTES AGO AND SUDDENLY IT'S A GREAT IDEA

WHEN YOU'RE CLEARING THE DISHES AND
YOUR FINGER TOUCHES SOME OF THE FOOD

MUM: WHO IS RESPONSIBLE FOR THIS MESS

US:

WHEN YOU SEE PEOPLE MAKING PLANS WITHOUT YOU

GETTING HOME AND FINALLY
BEING ABLE TO BINGE-WATCH
YOUR FAVOURITE SERIES

WHEN YOU'RE HOME ALONE AND HEAR A NOISE FROM THE OTHER ROOM

WHEN YOU'VE BEEN IN THE SHOWER FOR 40 MINUTES AND YOU'RE PERFORMING THE ENCORE TO YOUR STADIUM TOUR

THEM: DON'T JUMP TO ANY CONCLUSIONS
ME:

WHEN YOU FINISH
THE LAST EPISODE
OF A SERIES AND
THEN DON'T KNOW
WHAT TO DO
WITH YOURSELF

FEELING LIKE A PHOTOGRAPHER AFTER TAKING ONE DECENT PHOTO OF THE SUNSET

WHEN THE SUN COMES OUT FOR 5 SECONDS

EXPLAINING THE COMPLEX STORYLINE OF YOUR FAVOURITE SERIES TO YOUR FRIENDS

MY CRUSH: LOL THIS ISN'T A DATE

ME:

WHEN A TALL PERSON STANDS TOO CLOSE TO YOU

ME MASQUERADING AS
A FUNCTIONING ADULT

BAE: CAN I TRY SOME OF YOUR FOOD?
ME:

WHEN BESTIE GOES ON HOLIDAY WITHOUT ME

WHEN SOMEONE TAKES
A PHOTO WITHOUT
ME KNOWING

TRYING TO FEEL
COMFORTABLE
IN FORMAL
CLOTHES

WHEN SOMEONE
HAS TO EXPLAIN
SOMETHING FOR
THE FIFTH TIME
AND I STILL
DON'T GET IT

WHEN YOU HIT YOUR TOE ON THE TABLE LEG

SITTING AT THE WINDOW AND WAITING FOR PIZZA THREE SECONDS AFTER ORDERING IT ONLINE

WHEN YOU'RE SHOPPING ONLINE AND THE TOTAL COMES TO THREE TIMES THE AMOUNT IN YOUR BANK ACCOUNT

WHEN YOU'RE WATCHING A FILM
AND CAN'T WORK OUT WHERE
YOU'VE SEEN THAT ACTOR BEFORE

REALISING YOU LEFT YOUR SNACK IN THE KITCHEN JUST AFTER YOU GOT COMFY ON THE SOFA

WHEN YOU TEXT SOMEONE IN THE SAME ROOM AS YOU AND YOU SIT THERE WAITING FOR THEM TO NOTICE

WHEN YOU'RE STARVING AND FINALLY
ABOUT TO EAT SOMETHING DELICIOUS

IMAGE CREDITS

If you're interested in finding out more about our books, find us on Facebook at **Summersdale Publishers** and follow us on Twitter at **@Summersdale**.

www.summersdale.com